LIFE AFTER DEATH:

HEAVEN AND HELL ARE REAL PLACES

JACQUI D. WILLIAMS

LIFE AFTER DEATH:

HEAVEN AND HELL ARE REAL PLACES

JACQUI D. WILLIAMS

Christian Faith
PUBLISHING

ISBN 979-8-89130-068-2 (paperback)
ISBN 979-8-89130-069-9 (digital)

Christian Faith Publishing
832 Park Avenue
Meadville, PA 16335
www.christianfaithpublishing.com

All scriptures are taken from the KING JAMES VERSION (KJV): KING JAMES VERSION, public domain.

Printed in the United States of America

To my husband, in our many conversations, your compassion for the unsaved continues to bless my heart. I was inspired to write this book to remind everyone there is life after death, and you can have peace when your life is surrendered to Jesus Christ.

CONTENTS

CHAPTER 1

An Appointed Time

There is a season and a time for every purpose under heaven. A time to love and a time to hate, a time of war and a time of peace, a time to be born and a time to die (Ecclesiastes 3:1–8). Every person has an appointed time when they will depart from this earth. This is our death date. Sadly, many are living their lives as though they could care less about what happens to their soul after death. If you see no need for a Savior who can cleanse, deliver, and save you, then you will see no need to repent and receive Jesus as Lord. However, whether you accept Jesus or not, after death, your eternity is determined by the decision you make.

You and I both know there are some who care nothing about God nor care anything about giving their life to the Lord. They only believe in the here and now and think that this is all there is to life; so why not eat, drink, and be merry? But there is something more, and when death comes, we will leave our body in its shell, and our spirit will leave to enter either heaven or hell. Many then will wish they would have taken the time to accept Jesus as Lord. Let me tell you now before your death date arrives, while you are still living and have breath in your body, you have time. However, if you like living on the edge and feel you can wait until you are on your deathbed before you call out to the Lord, then that is your choice. Even if you want to risk your soul by accepting Jesus at the very end of your life, God will still be right there. Although it is far better to call on Him while you are able because no one knows what state they may find themselves in at the end. If you are a split second past your death date, then you will be a split second too late.

> *For man also knoweth not his time: as the fishes that are taken in an evil net, and as the birds that are caught in the snare; so are the sons of men snared in an evil time, when it falleth suddenly upon them. (Ecclesiastes 9:12)*

One thing that seems to bring everyone back to reality is death. We all know that when death happens to someone close in our life, this is the one time we remember how our life here on earth is not permanent. We start to think about what will happen to us when our life comes to an end. Some wonder if they will ever see their loved ones again after this life is over. The truth is, some will see their loved ones again and some will not. Why? Because there will be a separation from those who have given their life to the Lord and those who have not. This separation is called heaven and hell. These are two separate places based on two separate decisions made while we were living on earth. We either accepted Jesus or rejected Jesus as the Lord of our life. The Bible assures us in 1 Thessalonians 4:16–18, where it reads, *"For the Lord himself shall descend from heaven with a shout, with the voice of the archangel, and with the trump of God: and the dead in Christ shall rise first: Then we which are alive and remain shall be caught up together with them in the clouds, to meet the Lord in the air: and so shall we ever be with the Lord. Wherefore comfort one another with these words."*

Here, the Word of God lets us know that we will see our loved ones again if we have received Jesus as our Lord and Savior. We as believers know Jesus will return, and with great expectancy, we watch and wait. Not even the angels in heaven nor Jesus know the time of when that return will be. Only God Himself has set the appointed time (Matthew 24:36). We do not need to know the day or the hour, but what we do know is, every day, we get a little closer to His return than the day before, and we must remain ready at all times. Therefore, we can confirm from the Bible that everything on earth has its own appointed time according to God's plan, and we can rest in knowing we will spend our eternity in heaven with those who have received Jesus as Lord.

In 1 Corinthians 11:1, it reads, *"Be ye followers of me, even as I also am of Christ."* And in Jeremiah 17:5, it states, *"Thus saith the LORD; Cursed be the man that trusteth in man, and maketh flesh his arm, and whose heart departeth from the LORD."* The Bible is clear here that we are to place no trust in the arm of the flesh (man) and to only follow someone as they follow Christ. I love this because it takes the pressure off the need to feel like we must trust people. Nowhere in the Bible does it say for us to trust people. It only says we are to trust God. People do not have the power nor the capability to deliver us, change us, or save us. Sure, we can trust people to a degree but not to the point that they become the be-all and end-all answer to our happiness or joy. People will fail you in some way, no matter how hard they try not to. Why is that? Because no person can supply our every need. They are not meant to.

God is our provider and the only source for whom we can place complete trust and confidence in. He knows the beginning and ending of our every circumstance and situation. Satan would love for you to believe that a person can fulfill your deepest heart's desires, but no man or woman can ever do this. The devil wants us to be distracted by other people so he can use that opportunity to pull us away from following God. The devil knows God is the only one who can be everything to us because God created us, not people. If Satan can get us to feel inadequate or to make us think that we are missing out on something, then we will continue to be disappointed, upset, and unfulfilled in our life.

God knows all things, including our death date. This means that nobody dies before their time. Have you ever felt like someone may have died before their time? Whether that was twenty-two years or twenty-two minutes; however long we may live on this earth, when we die, it was our appointed time. The Word of God says not one sparrow will fall to the ground without God knowing it. He knows how many hairs are on our heads, and He has us graven upon the palms of His hands. We can be certain that God will not get our death date confused. But what happens to babies and toddlers or those who cannot make a conscious decision on their own due to a mental disability? How is the accountability factor determined when their lack of mental capacity has a limitation on how they decide whether to follow Christ or not? Eternity for those persons will be based on the sovereignty of God.

According to the following scripture, it is clear that children will not be hindered to enter heaven as we see here in Matthew 19:14, *"But Jesus said, Suffer little children, and forbid them not, to come unto me: for of such is the kingdom of heaven."* God's grace, through and by the blood and sacrifice that Jesus made on the cross for all sins, will cover them for eternity. You can trust in knowing that God will take care of those whom He knows cannot decide and make legitimate accountability decisions on their own.

"Even so it is not the will of your Father which is in heaven, that one of these little ones should perish" (Matthew 18:14).

Therefore, we can conclude, from God's Word, there is an appointed time for everyone and everything under the heavens. We can also conclude that no person will die before their time, and no one will leave this life too soon, no matter how old or young we believe them to be or what unfinished business we believe they have left behind. Their purpose on earth will have been completed. Of course, there may be things we wanted to do that we either did not get to do or did not finish before we died; but those are our plans, not necessarily God's plans. In some cases, God may have one person start a thing but has another person set up to finish it. As stated here in Psalm 75:7,

"But God is the judge: he putteth down one, and setteth up another." If God wants you to finish it, you will; but if it is not according to His purpose and plan, then your mission on earth is completed. God always gets accomplished what He needs to have accomplished, whether that be through you or someone else. So no need to despair. God has all of us set in place to fulfill whatever plan is needed for the earth; as we just read in the scripture above, God sets up, and God can bring down based on what He wants to have done.

Have you ever wondered if God could change your death date? Well, of course, we know He can, but whether He will or not will be determined based on His sovereignty. In 2 Kings 20, it shows that Hezekiah was very sick, and Isaiah the prophet was sent to him by God to let him know that he needed to get his house in order because his death was drawing near. Hezekiah then prayed heavily to the Lord, reminding Him how faithful he had been throughout his walk with God. The word of the Lord then came to Isaiah to go back to Hezekiah to let him know that God had heard his prayer, and He would heal him on the third day. Here in 2 Kings 20:5, it says, *"Turn again, and tell Hezekiah the captain of my people, Thus saith the LORD, the God of David thy father, I have heard thy prayer, I have seen thy tears: behold, I will heal thee: on the third day thou shalt go up unto the house of the LORD."* God then told Isaiah to inform Hezekiah that He will extend his days by fifteen years as seen here in 2 Kings 20:6, and it states, *"And I will add unto thy days fifteen years; and I will deliver thee and this city out of the hand of the king of Assyria; and I will defend this city for mine own sake, and for my servant David's sake."*

Therefore, we have the example, in Scripture, where God can and did change Hezekiah's death date by adding more years to his life span. Even though Hezekiah's appointed death date changed, it still happened years later. It may have been delayed, but it was not denied. At the end of 2 Kings 20:21, it says, *"And Hezekiah slept with his fathers: and Manasseh his son reigned in his stead."* We see here it mentions the death of Hezekiah came somewhere around the end of his fifteen years, just as God promised him.

Everything has its purpose and appointed time of completion on earth, and so do we. We know that Jesus's purpose was to teach, lead, guide, and to become a ransom for many by dying and shedding His blood on the cross. He provided a way that led us back to God so we could be reconciled with the Father. After Jesus accomplished His purpose, He died and ascended back to heaven. Jesus said in John 17:4, *"I have glorified thee on the earth. I have finished the work which thou gavest me to do."* All that we can see and touch will one day be no more; once it has fulfilled its purpose, it will end. When we face tough and difficult times, God comforts us through His Word and by surrounding us with the right people who will support us. It is good to know that even in our most difficult and trying times, even that is only temporary. Let us give thanks and praise to God because the last enemy to be destroyed is death. Yes, even death has its own death date and appointed time for when it will end. God's Word confirms that He will destroy death itself.

> *The last enemy that shall be destroyed is death. (1 Corinthians 15:26)*

CHAPTER 2

Where Will You Go after You Die?

When I hear that someone has died, one of the first things I say to myself is, "I pray their soul was saved." Why? Because this is the single most important thing we must do before we leave this earth, and that is to give our life to Jesus Christ. Jesus is the way, the truth, and the life, and He is our only way to God that will guarantee our entrance into heaven for all eternity (John 14:6). You can have money, life insurance, and a will, which are all good to have for your family who remains behind; but it will do nothing to secure your eternal soul. I implore anyone who has not received Jesus as the Lord of their life to receive Him as soon as possible. No one knows how long they will live, and once you have passed away, it will be too late to get your life in order.

There are not too many ways you can put it because there are only two realizations that matter, and that is do you receive Jesus as your Lord? Or do you reject Him and remain separated from God for all eternity? Have you ever wondered whether someone made it into heaven? Maybe you knew they were saved because they told you they gave their life to the Lord. I can tell you, according to the Bible, if they were saved, then you can be assured they are in heaven. But what about the person you think has lived a shady lifestyle? Does that mean they did not make it into heaven? Remember, only rejecting Jesus and failing to receive Him as your Lord is the only way you will not make it into heaven.

We are made righteous because we believe and accept the blood of Jesus Christ for the atonement of our sins, not only for our past sins but the present as well as any sins we commit in our future. When we turn our life over to Jesus, He will help us with our sinful behavior and wrong attitudes. However, for this to happen, you must give your life to Jesus so He can begin that good work in you. You cannot do this on your own; otherwise, God would not have sent His only Son to sacrifice His life on the cross.

In the Bible, it states that no adulterers, fornicators, idolaters, thieves, etc. will be able to enter the kingdom of heaven because none of these evils and wrongdoing can be tolerated in heaven. This is why we need to receive Jesus as our Savior before we die because if we do not, there is no cleansing from our sins that can allow us to enter in. It is only the blood of Jesus that washes away our sins for our past, present, and future. Our sins are stained like scarlet, and only Jesus can make them white as snow as it states here in Isaiah 1:18, *"Come now, and let us reason together, saith the Lord; though your sins be as scarlet, they shall be as white as snow; though they be red like crimson, they shall be as wool."*

The Word of God says that we are the righteousness of God through Christ Jesus our Lord. We are not righteous because we have led a sinless life or because we have maintained an impeccable right behavior. There is no way we could make it past twenty-four hours without doing something wrong, and there is nothing we can do that stamps our good deeds as righteousness before the King of kings. The Word of God says our righteousness is as filthy rags as stated here in Isaiah 64:6, *"But we are all as an unclean thing, and all our righteousnesses are as filthy rages; and we all do fade as a leaf, and our iniquities, like the wind, have taken us away."* Even based on what we would think to be our best day as being a *"good person"* still would not justify as being good enough to make it into heaven on our own merits. Only Jesus's blood can wash away the nastiness of our sinful ways that can redeem us to be able to stand before the presence of God.

> *For he hath made him to be sin*
> *for us, who knew no sin; that we*

might be made the righteousness of God in him. (2 Corinthians 5:21)

Have you ever heard someone say at a funeral, "Oh, poor so and so" as if the dead should be pitied. Well, I have, and I thought to myself at that moment, *The only way I could possibly understand that kind of thinking is if you knew for certain the person deceased was not saved.* Which, by the way, no one really knows that for sure. None of us can be certain if a person did or did not give their life to the Lord before they took their last breath. Only God knows if a person is sincere in wanting Him or just making a last attempt to escape hell. No one knows the true intentions of a person's heart. Every person will stand before the Lord and give an account for deeds done in their own body; and trust me, you will not be able to help anyone else nor will they be able to help you. We must make our own decisions and choices based on our own beliefs and faith in God. We can only trust and hope that, in the end, the ones we love and hold dear to our hearts have done the same. Share the good news of the Gospel of Jesus Christ whenever you can so others can have the chance to know the truth and make the right choice.

> *For whosoever shall call upon the name of the Lord shall be saved. (Romans 10:13)*

When a person you know dies, and, to the best of your knowledge, you believe that they were saved, then you can have peace and assurance that they have entered heaven. We who remain will miss them, but we can rejoice also in knowing that, without a doubt, they are rejoicing in heaven with the Lord and with all those who have gone before them. This is why we celebrate the life they lived here on earth and rejoice for those who have entered their heavenly bliss for all eternity as stated in Revelation 21:4, "*And God shall wipe away all tears from their eyes; and there shall be no more death, neither sorrow, nor crying, neither shall there be any more pain: for the former things are passed away."*

Satan wants people to get caught up with nonconcerning matters so they can miss out on what does matter, and that is getting your life right with the Lord. I do not know, but maybe those people who reject God don't believe He really exists or think that Satan and hell aren't real. If they don't, they will be in for a serious rude awakening. You can see the enemy working through people in so many ways from the evil deeds done through mass shootings, wars between countries, racism on all levels, lies that provoke wrongdoing, and the failure to hold others accountable.

> *A false witness shall not be unpunished, and he that speaketh lies shall not escape. (Proverbs 19:5)*

Most of us can probably remember this cult back in the 1970s that had people hooked on the lies that eventually led them to their deaths. I am sure they probably never thought that would happen or that it could go that far, but they believed in a man more than they believed in the truth of God's Word. It is critical that you read the Word of God for yourself and pray for His Holy Spirit to open and give you understanding of what God is speaking to you. Otherwise, cults, false prophets and teachings, or anyone promoting lies will have the open door to lead you astray. Remember, cult leaders do not usually come out and say, "I am a cult leader." If they did, hopefully you would remove yourself from the situation. But if you continue to be connected and follow their lies, you will succumb to their destruction.

God's Word is truth and will always guide us in the direction of what is truthful. However, we are responsible for receiving that truth, speaking that truth, and living that truth. If we keep our eyes on God and pray that we be not deceived by the enemy's lies, God will make certain that we are guided in the right direction. Where God is, there is truth, and where truth is, there will always be God's liberty and freedom in our life. Remember, Jesus Christ is the way, the truth, and the life. If you do not think you need Jesus to save you, you are free to think that way, but when your end comes, you will find out. Please know that whether people believe in Jesus or not, they will still bow their knees to Him in the end. As the Scripture says in Philippians 2:10–11, every knee shall bow and every tongue shall confess that Jesus Christ is Lord. We who love, honor, and believe in Jesus, freely and lovingly bow our knees and confess Jesus as Lord. However, to those who do not believe now, at the end will still bow their knees to the one who sits at the right hand of God the Father and Creator of all heaven and earth. Whether you bow now or not to Jesus, you will bow later.

> *Wherefore God also hath highly exalted him, and given him a name which is above every name. (Philippians 2:9)*

Satan knows the Scriptures probably better than we do. He knows God is all powerful, he knows Jesus is Lord, and he knows his end is coming. He wants to bring along with him as many as he can to be in torment with him. Satan would love for you to not believe in God, Jesus, heaven, hell, or himself. Satan is banking on that you will be completely deceived, and he is hoping you will fail to receive Jesus as the Lord of your life. If you do not receive Jesus, then you are on the track that the devil wants you to be, and that track will lead you straight to hell along with him. This is the big lie, and Satan is the father of lies and the master behind every lie ever told. When you hear a lie, know that it is ultimately Satan who is the origin behind that lie, and its purpose is to destroy and lead you to death. Satan has got his hooks around people's necks, hoping they will believe the falsehoods that cause them to believe that good is evil, and evil is good as we read here in Isaiah 5:20, *"Woe unto them that call evil good, and good evil; that put darkness for light, and light for darkness; that put bitter for sweet, and sweet for bitter!"* This is another sign in the Bible that we are to be watchful, for that signifies we are getting closer to the end times.

> *Be sober, be vigilant; because your adversary the devil, as a roaring lion, walketh about, seeking whom he may devour. (1 Peter 5:8)*

CHAPTER 3

Why Do Bad Things Happen to Seemingly Good People?

Life, with its unexpected situations and circumstances, can leave us wondering, *What in the world is happening?* Or maybe you may have thought, *Why me or why Ms. Johnson? She is such a sweet and loving woman.* Why would God allow this to happen to whom we would think, in our opinion, to be a seemingly *good person.* We should not be so quick to arrive at the notion of what we may conclude as a *good person.* Our first impressions are based mostly on what we see from the outward appearance, which tells us nothing of the true inside of a person. Only God knows our true hearts and intentions. But whether we think people are good or not, the Bible tells us in Romans 3:12, *"They are all gone out of the way, they are together become unprofitable; there is none that doeth good, no, not one."* In Psalm 14:3, it says, *"They are all gone aside, they are all together become filthy: there is none that doeth good, no, not one."*

Here we have two separate places in the Bible saying pretty much the same thing. There is no one good; no, not one. Okay, so we should be clear on this fact, but we still hear and find ourselves making these *good person* statements as to why we think they are too *good* for bad things to happen. Yet, things still happen, and things will continue to happen. Why? Because the Bible also states that God makes his sun to rise on the evil and on the good and sends rain on the just and the unjust (Matthew 5:45). In short, God is no respecter of persons; meaning there is no favoritism with God as mentioned in Romans 2:11, *"For there is no respect of persons with God."*

Life happens to all of us, good and bad, and none of us are exempt from life's challenges and storms. Jesus tells us that in the world, we will have trials and tribulations, but be of good cheer because He has overcome the world (John 16:33), and so can we. We can do all things through Christ who strengthens us (Philippians 4:13). When bad things do happen, don't think it is because God is mad at you or punishing you for some past wrongdoing; God does not operate this way. God knows our appointed time, and when it happens is something that nobody has the answer to but God because He is omniscient and has knowledge of all things. We have heard of tragic accidents and car crashes where people have walked away, and some people who have gotten sick with the same illness and have lived for years after, while others may die within months. Why does this happen? And why did it have to happen that way? The only answer I can give is, once again, it was their appointed time. This is one appointment none of us will be late for nor can we RSVP that we will not be able to attend. We do not set it nor can we control it, for it has already been predetermined before we were even born.

God is open for any questions we may have; however, if you are questioning His sovereignty or power, you are already off track, and just because you are asking God a question does not mean He will give you the answer right away or at all. There are some things we do not need to know; one reason is because, more than likely, we could not handle the answer. The times when we want to know why something happened the way it did, when God wants us to know, He will make it clear to us when the time is right. It may be years before we understand the reasons why something happened the way it did, and sometimes the answer may be given to us moments after we have asked. However, I do know, either way, if it is for us to know, God will make sure we have the answer when we need it. Otherwise, do not concern yourself with the why and the how come because God always has our best interest in mind.

*And this is the confidence that
we have in him, that, if we ask
any thing according to his will,
he heareth us. (1 John 5:14)*

When I was around twenty-six years of age, my mother found out she had lung cancer. We were devasted and hurting on the inside. Our family was heavily in prayer for God to work a miracle on her behalf. We were praying for the manifestation of her healing and that the cancer would be totally removed from her body. We knew, by the stripes of Jesus, she was already healed, and the evidence of her manifestation was on the way. Nobody wants to see someone they love go through the pain and agony of any illness. God's ways are not our ways, and God's timing is not our timing. It is hard to believe, but our relationship with God grows whenever our faith is tested because it is during trials we learn patience. This was a very difficult time, and God's strength helped us to move forward one day to the next, and through this, we gained experience with God.

On Sunday morning, May 6, 1990, shortly after midnight, my mother passed on into glory and entered the presence of God. We all knew then she had received her healing in its full manifestation. We were hurt and did not understand why her healing came through the result of her death. We were perplexed but at the same time knew she was beaming with unspeakable joy because she was now forever in the presence of God where there is no sickness, disease, or pain of any kind. I know God, in all His sovereignty, knew what was best for her and us at that time. God did answer our prayers, but not the way we thought or wanted Him to. All I can say is that I know my mother has stepped into her eternity and has the kind of joy that we cannot even begin to comprehend while here on earth. Remember, to live is Christ, but to die is gain; so, either way, it is a win-win situation.

And we know that all things work together for good to them that love God, to them who are the called according to his purpose. (Romans 8:28)

God is omniscient, which means He has complete knowledge, awareness, and understanding of all things; and only God knows what is best for us. Since God is already in our tomorrows, He already knows what we need and what lies before us in our future. Which brings me back to the first chapter of this book, "An Appointed Time." It was my mother's appointed time to die, and the best part out of this whole thing is that my mother was a born-again, Spirit-filled believer, who not only dedicated but also gave her life to serving Jesus Christ as her personal Lord and Savior. It is only by God's grace and mercies that we wake up day after day, and some did not wake up today, and some will not wake up tomorrow. Some of us are graced to live for ninety-five years, and some are only graced to live for five years. Since we do not know how long our years will be on this earth, it is best to make the most of the opportunity you have today.

In 2 Corinthians 6:2, it says today is the day of salvation. This is letting us know that we only have today to receive Jesus as our Lord and Savior, and there is no guarantee that another day of life will be offered to us to make that decision. If you are thinking you have plenty of time and can put off receiving Jesus for another day, then you are taking a gamble with your life. Our life can end at any moment. Life is like a balloon that floats in the air, and once the air is gone, its shell withers to the ground. One day, we are here, and another day, we are gone. By no means is this to make light of our hurt and pain. It is meant to remind us to try and keep an attitude of gratitude, when going through hard times, by reflecting on the everyday blessings that are right in front of us. We do not want to miss the good things that God is doing in our midst by allowing the struggles to overshadow His daily goodness to us. Be intentional about keeping a heart of thanksgiving to God, in and through all things, by trusting that He can and will bring good out of our every situation in some way.

> *Whereas ye know not what shall be on the morrow. For what is your life? It is even a vapour, that appeareth for a little time, and then vanisheth away. (James 4:14)*

CHAPTER 4

The Devil: The Reason for the Evil in the World

Every evil, disgusting, and hurtful thing that you can think of, present in the world today, is a result of the fall of man. Evil entered the world through the disobedience of the first man (Adam). In the garden of Eden, the serpent (Satan) manipulated and deceived Eve (the first woman) into thinking that they were missing out on something big by not having the freedom to eat all the fruit that God had placed within the garden. The devil, through his cunning and deceptive ways, told Eve that they would not die if they ate the fruit, but that they would become more like gods.

> *And he said unto the woman, Yea, hath God said, Ye shall not eat of every tree of the garden? And the woman said unto the serpent, We may eat of the fruit of the trees of the garden: But of the fruit of the tree which is in the midst of the garden, God hath said, Ye shall not eat of it, neither shall ye touch it, lest ye die. And the serpent said unto the woman, Ye shall not surely die: For God doth know that in the day ye eat thereof, then your eyes shall be opened, and ye shall be as gods, knowing good and evil. (Genesis 3:1–5)*

Satan's primary goal was to persuade Eve to be disobedient to God, hoping Adam would follow behind her. I would say that it probably was not so much about the fruit itself, but more so about the fact that they disobeyed God by doing what God said not for them to do. When Adam failed to obey the command given to him by God, this opened the door which allowed the evil (sin) to come into the world. The following scripture is what God spoke to Adam in Genesis 2:16–17, and it states, *"And the LORD God commanded the man, saying Of every tree of the garden thou mayest freely eat: But of the tree of the knowledge of good and evil, thou shalt not eat of it: for in the day that thou eatest thereof thou shalt surely die."*

All of mankind died in that moment because of the first man's (Adam) failure to obey what God had commanded him not to do. If you read Genesis 2 and 3, you can see that the command to not eat the fruit was given to Adam, not Eve. Therefore, when Eve first ate the fruit from the tree of the knowledge of good and evil, sin did not enter at that moment; sin entered the moment after she gave the fruit to Adam, and he did eat of that fruit. God then called out to Adam first, then to Eve to confront what they had done (Genesis 3:9, 13).

The bad and evil things happening in the world today should be no surprise based on the scriptures we have read throughout the Bible. It informs us of the evils that are to come and that are already here. Scanning through past generations and fast forwarding to present day, we can see times have gotten worse, and as time goes on, according to the Bible, it will continue. Therefore, it is important that we share the Gospel whenever and wherever possible. But one of the best ways to share is simply through our own daily lifestyle for others to see. I love the saying *"Your life may be the only Bible some people will ever read."* This is letting us know that it is up to all of us, who call ourselves believers of Jesus Christ, to not just talk about it but live it as well.

In Psalm 33:5, it says, *"He loveth righteousness and judgment: the earth is full of the goodness of the Lord."* Even though sin entered the world through the disobedience of man (Adam) in the beginning, the earth is still full of the goodness of the Lord. We, as believers, must do our part by letting our light shine so others can see our good works and glorify God. As it reads here in Matthew 5:16, *"Let your light so shine before men, that they may see your good works, and glorify your Father which is in heaven."*

It seems that the devastation of earthquakes, hurricanes, and tornadoes still gets mentioned at times as acts of God. Do you know that when God created the world, He created it perfect, and everything in it was beautiful and at peace? This was until Satan began thinking that he could be like God and tried to usurp His authority by seeking to overthrow God's power. From that moment on, Satan has continued to lie and continued to seek whomever he can devour to suffer with him in an everlasting punishment that can never be escaped. Satan is a liar, and the father of lies, and he would love for us to conceal the truth of a matter so he can continue to torture us and keep us in bondage.

When you lie, you generally have to keep lying to cover your tracks. The problem with that is it becomes harder to keep your story straight. But when you tell the truth, you do not have to worry about having a good memory because the truth never changes. It is always best that when you feel yourself getting ready to tell a lie, just bust yourself out and say, *"You know what? I'm lying."* After you do that a few times, you will free yourself. Also, it is only in telling the truth and being truthful with yourself and others that you will ever be truly free. Healing and restoration can only begin when you are truthful. Just remember, lying is just what Satan wants you to do so you can remain in his prison. When you tell the truth, it exposes the enemy right up-front, and your deliverance and healing can begin.

> *And ye shall know the truth, and*
> *the truth shall make you free.*
> *(John 8:32)*

We should be able to conclude now that the evils in the world today are a result of sin that entered the world due to the fall of Adam.

However, the consequences that we find our-selves in come from our own personal choices that we make and fail to take responsibility and accountability for. We must allow the Holy Spirit of God to give us the power to overcome temptation. Although our actions may be pro-voked by the enemy (the devil), it is still our decision whether we follow it through.

In Joshua 24:15, it says, *"Choose you this day whom ye will serve."* This should be clear for us to see that the choices we make for what we do and say produce the results, and we must assume full responsibility. All the hatred, racism, murders, mass shootings, robberies, stealing, etc. are evils in the world from us who partake in them, and it will con-tinue to make an evil world that is generated by the disobedience of man. Therefore, the next time we hear someone even coming close to blaming the evil tragedies and misfortunes on God, by saying, *"Well, that was an act of God,"* you can remember this: evil entered the world because of the influence of Satan, but it continues because of the disobedience of man, not God.

CHAPTER 5

Heaven and Hell Are Real Places

Many have given their recollections of near-death experiences, accounts, dreams, and visions of their brief visits to heaven and hell. First, I want to talk about John who bares record of the Word of God and the testimony of Jesus Christ from the things which he saw that are written in the book of Revelation, which further confirms to me that heaven and hell are real places. Just to be clear on what I discuss here in this book, I would never assume or dare to attempt to add nor take away from John's account but only to take joy in how John was able to witness and write down his account of all that was revealed to him by the angel of the Lord. I would encourage you to read the book of Revelation in its entirety to better comprehend for yourself what the Spirit of God wants to show you. I would imagine John's overwhelming honor to be chosen by God to witness the things that are shortly to come to pass as we see here in Revelation 1:1, which states, *"The Revelation of Jesus Christ, which God gave unto him, to shew unto his servants things which must shortly come to pass; and he sent and signified it by his angel unto his servant John."*

I cannot understand how some find it hard to believe that there is a heaven or hell but have no problem in believing in UFOs or the possibility of life on other planets or that you can come back in another lifetime as an animal or another person. I pray by me writing this book that it can be a help in some way to those who may not yet believe but will come to know that heaven and hell are real places. The decision you make now while you are still living, to receive or reject Jesus as

Lord, will determine where you spend eternity after your death.

Hell is a place of constant torment, gnashing of teeth, crawling worms that never die, and an ever-burning furnace fire that will never go out. It will have the stench of melting skin, echoing sounds of wailing cries that are compounded by the fear in knowing that this is their final destination. Hell is a place of everlasting punishment where there is no rest, day or night. Hell is not a place of fun, parties, and freedom to sin any way you want with friends. I don't know how anyone could possibly think that way, since all the accounts of hell on record that are noted in Scripture—fun, parties, and freedom to sin are not on the list.

After death, if your fate is sealed for hell, you will spend eternity in excruciating torment where you will have no chance of ever getting out. In hell, the punishment continues and has no end in sight to its devastation. Don't allow the enemy to trick you from the seriousness of your soul's eternity. In James

4:7, it says, *"Submit yourselves therefore to God. Resist the devil, and he will flee from you."* The biggest mistake you could ever make is to reject Jesus as Lord for your life or to believe that you will have time to get things right with God later in your life. There are no guarantees that anyone will have multiple opportunities to choose God later. Hell is not a joke to be played around with but should be taken seriously.

> *And shall cast them into the furnace of fire: there shall be wailing and gnashing of teeth. (Matthew 13:50)*

This is not just me saying this to you; this is from the Word of God, and His Word is faithful and true. Don't think that when believers talk about hell that we are trying to use a scare tactic to make people believe in God. God's Word is about His love for us that allows us the opportunity to experience the joy He has prepared for those who choose to believe in Him. If it scares you, I would say there is nothing to be scared about because God gives you a choice. If you are the one who controls the outcome of where you go for eternity, then why would you be scared? This is great news how God has given us the freedom of choice. God is awesome in the way He gives us the choice because when you think about it, all of us deserve to go straight to hell, no shortcuts or detours, but straight to hell. He did not have to give us a choice, but He did, and for that alone, we should all be grateful to Him for His awesome freedom of choice.

We are all sinners, and the only thing that stops me and you from going to hell is the choice we make to place our faith in Jesus Christ alone. But just a note from what I have read in the Scriptures, it looks to me that hell is the worst horror film you could ever image; so if that scares you, then that fear you have would be valid.

And the smoke of their torment ascendeth up for ever and ever: and they have no rest day nor night, who worship the beast and his image, and whosoever receiveth the mark of his name. (Revelation 14:11)

Heaven is only for those who have surrendered their life with gladness to the Lord Jesus Christ. It is an open and freewill choice for all to make, but not many feel the need to be a part of the family of God, until it is too late. The one thing that we all can agree on is this, that our end will come one day. We as believers are hoping to bring as many as we can to heaven with us. I love the scripture in 1 Corinthians 2:9, and it states, *"But as it is written, Eye hath not seen, nor ear heard, neither have entered into the heart of man, the things which God hath prepared for them that love him."* We do not serve God because we have to. We serve God because we want to and because we are thankful for all He has done for us. If it is hard for you to serve God or pains you to give Him praise and worship, then examine whether you are sincere and true in your walk and relationship with Him.

Over the years, I can remember two dreams I had that only quickly gave me a gentle touch of what I believe was the peace and beauty of heaven. I will only share this one dream I had several years ago. This one I believe was more distinctive and possibly was my glimpse of heaven. It was a quick dream to start, and I was with my brother, Tyrone. We were walking along this riverbank, which to me seemed kind of odd. I remember my brother was trying to get me to step over to the other side, and I did not want to do it. I said to him, "So if I step over to this other side with you, does that mean I will be in heaven? And if I go with you over to the other side, doesn't that mean that I will be dead on earth as I know it to be now?"

He said, "Yes, but it will be okay because you will step over into heaven."

I paused, and I then took his hand, and I went to step over, and then suddenly I was in what was supposed to be heaven, and it was simply beautiful! It was a quick glimpse, and I cannot begin to explain to you what I saw. All I know is it was beautiful! As soon as I stepped over into what I thought in my dream to be heaven, I woke up. I was puzzled by that dream when I woke up because at that time, my brother was living and not to my knowledge was even sick.

Fast forwarding, years later, when my brother called to tell me he was sick, it bothered me for a while because I never forgot that dream. In the dream, he was already passed and was letting me know that it was okay to step over into heaven. He already knew that heaven was a beautiful and peaceful place to be in, and I should not be afraid to leave this earth when I die. The dream to me was a form of confirmation that when my appointed time comes, and I cross over into heaven that I know that I will be in a much better place than I could ever experience while here on earth. Even though my brother has been deceased for over eleven years, I rest in knowing that he is in the presence of the Lord I know my brother was born again and Jesus was the Lord of his life, so the dream does not confirm where he is to me. I already know where he is because of what the Word of God says.

Dreams can help to bring further peace in what we already know, but please do not get overly excited because you had a dream. Be more excited because you believe God's Word and honored that He has chosen to bless you in this way. God will reveal secrets to us through and by His Holy Spirit, just as it states throughout the scriptures.

> *The secret of the LORD is with them that fear him; and he will shew them his covenant. (Psalm 25:14)*

> *Even the mystery which hath been hid from ages and from genera-*

*tions, but now is made manifest
to his saints. (Colossians 1:26)*

My point to all of this is that I want people to know that it is okay for us to cry and miss the ones who have passed on. But after the tears, wipe them away, and rejoice with them, knowing they are stress-free, drama-free, and way better off than we could ever imagine. They are already experiencing their eternity with no sickness, pain, or sorrows that comes along with living in this present world. Jesus has overcome the world, and Jesus has prepared a place for all of those who believe and place their trust in Him. We will experience our complete bliss one day in the future, and God will make certain that our transition will be a peaceful and joyous one for all those who believe in Him.

I place no confidence in the dreams I had or will have. God has blessed me with some beautiful dreams, and yes, I know God has and can speak to me in that way if He so chooses. But I caution anyone to not ever place your sole confidence in a dream, prophecy, or anything other than the Word of God. You do not want to get off track by trying to figure out what this dream meant or waiting for a prophet to give you a word for your life. True, God can speak to you in a dream and through a prophet to give you a word, but you never want to miss what God is saying to you first in His written Word. As it states here in Matthew 24:35, *"Heaven and earth shall pass away, but my words shall not pass away."* We know that throughout the Bible, God has used dreams to get a message to people, and two of them I can recall. One was when the angel of the Lord appeared to Joseph in a dream to let him know it was okay to take Mary as his wife. The angel advised Joseph that the child that Mary was carrying was conceived from the Holy Spirit in Matthew 1:20, and it says, *"Joseph son of David, do not be afraid to take Mary home as your wife, because what is conceived in her is from the Holy Spirit."* The second one was when God showed another Joseph in a dream that he would rule over his brothers and they would later bow down to him, found in Genesis 37:5, and it states, *"And Joseph dreamed a dream, and he told it his brethren: and they hated him yet the more."*

We can clearly see where God has no problem speaking to you or me in a vision or a dream if He wants to get a message to us. However, our primary confidence should always be in what God speaks to us through His already written Word and by our personal conversations we have with Him in prayer. I only shared my dream to show another example of how my experiences with God reveal to me what I already believed through His Word, and that is heaven and hell are real places.

> *And he said, Hear now my words:*
> *If there be a prophet among you,*
> *I the LORD will make myself known unto him in a vision, and will speak unto him in a dream. (Numbers 12:6)*

CHAPTER 6

God Will Respect Our Choice

God is love, and all that He has shown us throughout the Bible and through the ages is His great love for all mankind. But what we should also know and appreciate is the free will that God gives to each person. We were not made to be robots. God wants us to love Him on our own, serve Him on our own, and come to Him on our own, and if you so choose not to serve Him and so choose not to receive His Son Jesus Christ as the Lord and Savior of your life; then yes, God will respect your choice, and yes, respect your right and choice to go straight to hell.

I am sure you have heard at some point in your life that if God is love, and He is, then He will not let us go to hell. I am sure you have also heard that in the end, don't you think God will end up letting all of us into heaven? This kind of thinking will get you left behind if you are not careful, and, unfortunately, some will end up in hell for eternity simply because they believe in ideas just like this. They can't imagine that in all God's love and mercy, there is no way He will let us end up in such a horrible place. However, please understand that God is holy and just, and because He is holy, no evil or sin can be in His presence; and because He is just, He will not allow it. God is not a liar, and He will hold to His Word. God is not pushy, and He gives us the freedom to decide for ourselves who we want to serve. As we just discussed, God will allow your choice to carry you straight to hell if that is what you want to do.

> *And these shall go away into everlasting punishment: but*

the righteous into life eternal (Matthew 25:46)

Just a sidenote. It is important for you to know that there is no soul sleep or purgatory after death. We will step into our eternity the moment we die. Based on the decision we made while living on earth, our soul (spirit) will go immediately to its assigned destination the second after we have passed on. Our choice will result in us going to either heaven or hell. There is no in-between and no other place given in scripture for us to go. Hades, per Scripture, is spoken to be a place where the unrighteous souls (spirits) go to await their final judgment before being sentenced to hell for all eternity. One example, which speaks of hades, is found in Luke 16. Different translations say hell, others say hades. It is still in the lower parts of the earth where all your senses are still able to experience its horrible torment, and it is still not a place where you would want to be.

But don't think that if you go to hades before you are sentenced to hell that you have a chance to get things right with God. No, you will not. Your chances and choices are over. After death, then comes the judgment, and at the judgment, when God gives the final sentencing, then you will be sent to hell (the lake of fire) for all eternity. Hades is still hell, and there is a sentencing per the Scriptures that this is called the second death for the unrighteous souls, which is the final separation from God.

> *But the fearful, and unbelieving, and the abominable, and murderers, and whoremongers, and sorcerers, and idolaters, and all liars, shall have their part in the lake which burneth with fire and brimstone: which is the second death. (Revelation 21:8)*

I believe it is high time we speak the truth to people who wonder if you die a good person, can you still go to heaven? Or the person who you knew that clearly rejected God's ways, can they still make it in? The correct response for both scenarios would be no. We cannot hope or love someone into heaven by having wishful thoughts and loving feelings nor can anyone make it by their good intentions. None of these things will help anyone in the end after they have passed on. We must tell others the truth while they are living and have a fair chance to receive Jesus as the Lord of their life. This is the only way you can be assured of their entrance into heaven. Otherwise, we are all wasting valuable time not letting others know only for you to be later overwhelmed by their death, wondering what happened to their soul (spirit) in the end.

> *And whosoever was not found written in the book of life was cast into the lake of fire. (Revelation 20:15)*

Another note to remember: Attending church every week and serving faithfully in your assigned ministries does not guarantee your entrance into heaven. Remember, it is not our works that save us. It is only our acceptance of Jesus Christ into our hearts as our Lord and Savior that saves us from the eternal damnation of hell. Sometimes, you can get caught up into thinking that I am a good person, I am nice and respectful to others. For example, I do not rob or steal things that do not belong to me. I give to the poor and lend to the needy. I help others whenever I can. All these things are kind acts that are great to do, but you can still be a good-hearted person that is a nonbeliever on your way to hell because of your nonacceptance of Jesus Christ as your Lord.

I know my father, when I was much younger, took me to church with him on occasions, but my mother did not go. Then, later, as I got older, my father stopped going, and my mother started going, and once she started going to church, she never stopped.

I was led to believe that my father was not saved, even though he was the first one that I remember that went to church and not my mother. But somehow, we always associate a person who does not go to church as not being a believer. As I just mentioned above, going to church does not guarantee that you are saved, and let me also add that not going to church does not mean that you are not saved. Let me clarify, generally, when you are saved and a believer of Jesus Christ, you would want to go to learn more about how to live your life for God's glory and to understand His purpose for your life. But, for whatever reason, you and God only know the reason why some go to church and some do not.

But it is not for anyone to say, "Oh well, they are not saved because they do not go to church or yes, they are saved because they do go to church." Remember, it is not our actions or good or bad works that will keep us out of heaven. It is only our nonacceptance to receive Jesus Christ as our Lord and Savior that will send a person to hell. Not whether they attend or don't attend church.

After my mother passed in 1990, I had the joy and pleasure of spending more time getting to know my father on a much deeper level. I am here and happy to say, without a doubt, I know my father believed in God, and he did receive Jesus as the Lord and Savior of his life. Therefore, I know I will see him again in heaven along with my mother, brother, and other family and friends when my appointed time comes. My sister, Jan, made sure of this when my father was sick with cancer. She wanted to make certain that his soul was saved and right with the Lord. After talking with our father and confirming that he had accepted Jesus as His Lord, she later took communion with him, which I thought was so awesome for her to do. I know he was blessed by her doing that with him, and I was too. My sister, Jan, is a mission-ary who lives and ministers in Belize, Central America. I am so proud of her and appreciate the sacrifice she has made to live and serve God's people in another country.

> *And this gospel of the kingdom will be proclaimed throughout the whole world as a testimony to all nations, and then the end will come. (Matthew 24:14)*

Thankfully, all my siblings have a personal relationship with the Lord, and that is because of the prayers of our grandmother and parents whom I know were praying for us in the early years of our life. This is why I say it is important to bring your children up in the fear of God and to let them know about Jesus and the importance of getting their souls saved. My mother made sure all of us went to church every Sunday, and we as children did not have an option to stay home, and I am so thankful for that. I had it all around me, between my parents, grandparents, and my best friend's mother. I was always taught about the importance of receiving Jesus in my life. I do not think it is fair to let children go about their own way without pointing them in the direction they need to go, especially when it concerns their eternal souls. I believe we do anyone an injustice when we fail to give them the information that we know can help them toward having a better life.

As they grow older, they will decide on their own whether to receive Jesus as Lord, but always try to give some kind of foundation about God first. Otherwise, they end up not having anything solid to stand on when they are being directed in the wrong way in their early years of life. It is better to teach them when they are young so they are more equipped as they grow older. By the mercies of God, it can still be okay if you want to wait and take that chance, but in some cases, it is not okay, and sometimes you end up struggling and wrestling against so many different distractions and spirits that are in contradiction to the Word of God. You know and I know that it can be a whole lot harder trying to steer someone in the right direction once they are older, so why would you want to wait and take that chance?

> *Train up a child in the way he should go: and when he is old, he will not depart from it. (Proverbs 22:6)*

As I grew older, the desire to serve God grew and continues to grow stronger in me. I believe primarily because I was taught so young and it is in me and all of who I am as a person. Everybody makes their own personal decision when they get older, but they at least need to have the tools to know about Jesus so they can make a conscious decision on their own at whatever stage in life. If you think, *Well, I don't want to push them, so I will let them decide for themselves once they are older.* Nobody knows what will happen in someone's life, and you telling them about Jesus can be the turning point in how they handle what lies ahead. When you are their parent, guardian, or have children under your care, it is your responsibility to give that child all the proper tools you can to help them live their best life as they grow older. Just like you advise them about education, hygiene, etc. I would say teaching them about Jesus and living a life that honors God is much more important than anything else. Because when you have a relationship with the Lord, He will make sure everything else falls into place. Whatever you need, He can supply.

The Bible tells us in Matthew 6:33, *"But seek ye first the kingdom of God, and his righteousness; and all these things shall be added unto you."* I know for myself I had no interest in school growing up. The best part was seeing my friends in class. God helped and brought me through, and I have seen how He has brought me through every phase of my life. Therefore, I make sure I keep God top priority in all that I do, and I can see how all of what I need falls into place. Of course, I have had trials and tribulations along the way, like anyone else, but through it all, God continues to bring me through because I trust in Him to do so.

I would hate for you to put off receiving Jesus as your Lord until the last minute. However, even in that last minute is better than waiting until you have no minutes and your time here on earth is finished. Once you have passed on, it is over, and your fate is then sealed for all eternity. You will have no second chances to get it right with God later. Some might believe there will be another chance made available to them after death to receive Jesus. But there will be no other chance available. There is nowhere in Scripture that mentions second chances after death. The only second chances or opportunities that are made available are only while you are still living on earth.

In the Bible, God gave Jonah a second chance to do the right thing, and I am sure you can think and I know I can think of multiple times where God has not only given us a second chance but also a third, fourth, and so on chances to get it right. However, please note all those chances are made while there is still breath in our bodies. Once our journey on earth has ended, all our opportunities and chances will be over, and what we have chosen to do with our lives while we were still living will end. Once we die, there are no do-overs nor changes that can be made. Our death will end our story, and there will be nothing left to add or to remove from our life's history.

I love the way God gives us the freedom and choice to live any way we want to. God lets us know in His Word that there is a broad way and a narrow way of living, and we got options to decide which way we want. This way, in the end, nobody can blame anyone else, and especially we cannot blame God for the wrong individual choices we have made along the way. Some people go through life hating God because they say, "God took my wife or God took my child, etc."

Let me tell you now. You can stop hating God and blaming God for the death of your loved ones. Nobody has the right to blame God for a life taken when they had nothing to do with the creation of that life in the first place.

We were created for God's pleasure (Revelation 4:11), and we were made to serve and worship Him. But He still gives us the choice to come to Him on our own, and He does not make anybody worship and serve Him. He wants us to freely come to Him by our own choice. We choose to live our life the way we want. Some in a way with no regard or reverence to Him at all. Yet some operate as if they have rights of sole ownership. If you were the owner of something, your feelings would be understood in how you were thinking that God took something from you. But we entered this world with nothing, and we will leave with nothing. The Bible tells us: naked we came and naked we will return. God knows our hurt and pain over our lost loved ones, but do not blame God for taking what belongs only to Him.

Thankfully, God gives us the option to see our loved ones again within a perfect place that is free from pain, sickness, and death.

But until we realize that we are only here for His purpose and His glory, we will continue to waste our time thinking we were robbed from what He gave us only for a time and season to enjoy. Family, friends, and all that we are blessed to enjoy are a taste of the many gifts and pleasures God allows us to partake of while we are here on earth. Remember, we are not owners but stewards allowed to enjoy them for the time we have them. God is the giver and creator of life and only God has the power and right to take it away when the appointed time for it has come.

> *And said, Naked came I out of my mother's womb, and naked shall I return thither: the Lord gave, and the Lord hath taken away; blessed be the name of the Lord. (Job 1:21)*

CHAPTER 7

For All Eternity

Most of us have heard the phrase: we are only passing through on this earth, and our home is heaven. This is true for born-again believers who have received Jesus as the Lord and Savior of their life, but not true for those who reject Jesus Christ and have made the choice to live a life separated from God. Death only confirms that life here on earth as we know it will be over. Our body, the shell that we are presently living in, will go back to the dust that it was made from, as it states in Genesis 3:19, *"In the sweat of thy face shalt thou eat bread, till thou return unto the ground; for out of it wast thou taken: for dust thou art, and unto dust shalt thou return.*" Then our spirit will leave our body, and life will begin in our new destination for all eternity. In John 14:1–3, Jesus is speaking to His disciples, encouraging them to not be troubled but to rest in knowing that He will prepare a place for all who believe in Him.

> *Let not your heart be troubled: ye believe in God, believe also in me. In my Father's house are many mansions: if it were not so, I would have told you. I go to prepare a place for you. And if I go and prepare a place for you, I will come again, and receive you unto myself; that where I am, there ye may be also. (John 14:1–3)*

There is another destination prepared for those who have not received Jesus as Lord, and in the previous chapter, discussed from Revelation 20, anyone whose name is not found in the Book of Life was cast into hell-fire for all eternity, and again here in John 3:36, it reads, *"He that believeth on the Son hath everlasting life: and he that believeth not the Son shall not see life; but the wrath of God abideth on him."*

We should be preparing ourselves now, for our eternity, by setting up our treasures in heaven and not on earth. Meaning, our focus and goal should be winning souls to Christ for the good of God's eternal kingdom and direct our serving to His service and glorification. Also, did you know there will be rewards given to us in heaven? Yes, God says in His Word that He will reward us for deeds done on earth. Here in Colossians 3:24, it states, *"Knowing that of the Lord ye shall receive the reward of the inheritance: for ye serve the Lord Christ."* Please do not get this confused. Our works on earth do not and cannot, in any way, get us into heaven. However, our rewards will be based on our sincere love and service to God, and only God determines what that reward will be. God is already so good to us by giving us the opportunity to spend all eternity in heaven, and that alone already exceeds our highest expectations; and now we get rewards too! It just shows me how good and gracious God is to all of us.

I mentioned earlier how nonbelievers will die twice. The first death is the physical part of man, which is the shell (body) of a person that we see. Then in Revelation, it speaks about the second death. I want to explain this more. Your body has a soul and lives in a body, and death separates the body from the spirit. When you are saved, your spirit goes to live with God the moment you die; but when you are unsaved, your spirit will be separated from God for all eternity. This is the second death. In Romans 6:23, it says, *"For the wages of sin is death,"* and when you continue in your sin, it leads you to death if you fail to give your life to Jesus. Jesus is the only one who can free and deliver you from paying the wages that lead you to death for the second time. The first death we all will face when our appointed time comes, but the second death will only be experienced by nonbelievers due to their failure to accept Jesus Christ as their Lord.

Nonbelievers will get a double dose of death, twice as stated here in Revelation 20:13–14, *"And the sea gave up the dead which were in it; and death and hell delivered up the dead which were in them: and they were judged every man according to their works. And death and hell were cast into the lake of fire. This is the second death."* When you receive Jesus as Lord, you are accepting all that He has made available to us by the blood He shed on the cross. It is only the blood of Jesus that can wash away our sins. But when you reject Jesus as Lord, then you will experience total and final separation from God, which is the second death.

> *In whom we have redemption through his blood, the forgiveness of sins, according to the riches of his grace; (Ephesians 1:7)*

All of us are guilty of sin. Period. But the only thing that separates believers from nonbelievers is that believers have repented and placed their trust and faith in Jesus as Lord to cleanse them from their sins. Those who fail to repent and choose not to place their trust and faith in Jesus remain in their sin and are left with the guilt and sting of death as the penalty. Death has no sting when you are in Jesus as stated here in 1 Corinthians 15:55, "*O death, where is thy sting? O grave, where is thy victory?*" It is not a question of who is sinning or who is not sinning. We all have and do sin. But thanks be to God who has made a way for all of us to get cleansed from our sins. Therefore, there remains no excuse for anyone, and on that (judgment) day, when we stand before Him, if the blood of Jesus is not covering your sins, you will be damned to hell. I know saying it like that sounds bad, but there is no way to sugarcoat it nor should it ever be sugarcoated because trust me, going to hell, there is nothing sweet about it.

One thing you can be certain of is the choice you have right now to say yes or no to God. Nobody wants to be surprised at the end and discover they waited too late to receive Jesus as Lord. Of course, you have the right to take a risk with your eternity. I know as you read through this book, a lot of what I am saying sounds the same. Even to me, as I write, I find myself saying the same thing, but there are not too many other ways I can say it when you know how important it is to let someone know they need to give their life to the Lord. You want to engrave it into their minds that hell is not a place you want to be.

If you notice the same wording or the same phrases, it is only because I want to get the message across to the reader. I don't find that to be a bad thing because I know I am in good company. In the Word of God, you will read similar scriptures and points that are the same throughout the Bible. But I love when I see God repeating the same point because it lets me know that it is important to God; therefore, it should be important to us and shows it obviously bears repeating. Look at it this way, when you yell fire or scream for help, you don't do it one time. You more than likely will repeat it. Why? Because you want someone to hear you.

In Joshua 1:8, it reads, *"This book of the law shall not depart out of thy mouth; but thou shalt meditate therein day and night."* We should be meditating on the Word of God day and night. Meditation is a reflection with contemplation of thought, and when we practice with repetition, we will be able to repeat it over again. Whether you are reading it, hearing it, speaking it, or seeing it, you will produce the fruit that you have allowed yourself to meditate on. We should know by now that out of the abundance of our hearts, our mouths will speak. This can be good or bad, but you can believe that if you feed what is good on a regular basis, it is only natural for good fruit to come out of you; but when you repetitiously feed what is evil, you will produce bad fruit as a result.

> *Even so every good tree bringeth forth good fruit; but a corrupt tree bringeth forth evil fruit. (Matthew 7:17)*

Life can be long, but eternity is even longer, and where we spend eternity should matter to us. We realize that our physical bodies are slowly dying every day, and in the back of our minds, we know death is coming. For myself, being saved gives me peace and assurance knowing I will spend eternity in heaven with the Lord, and I will see my family and friends again who are saved as well. For everyone who reads this book, I hope they will grasp the urgency to do the same. If they have not yet chosen to believe in Jesus as their Lord, I pray they will receive Him before their end comes.

In the end, every believer and every non-believer, whom God has breathed life into will see Him as the one who lives, reigns, and sits on the throne forever and for all eternity. God has provided only one way to Him, and that is through and by His Son Jesus Christ. Jesus is our only hope for eternal life as seen here in John 17:3, *"And this is life eternal, that they might know thee the only true God, and Jesus Christ, whom thou hast sent."* You do not want to wait to the end of your life and find out that you missed out on your opportunity to receive Jesus Christ as Lord. Your fate for your eternity is sealed the moment you die. Many will hope for another chance to accept Jesus as Lord, and there will be none. God must and will honor His Word; and all non-believers (who have rejected His Son as Lord and King), the devil, and his angels will be cast into a hell of fire and brimstone for all eternity.

> *Then shall he say also unto them on the left hand, Depart from me, ye cursed, into everlasting fire, prepared for the devil and his angels: (Matthew 25:41)*

*Heaven and hell are determined by
the choice we make while
we are still living on earth.*

*Once our life has ended,
our eternity will be sealed,
and there will be no turning back.*

For those who desire God's gift of salvation, say this prayer with a sincere and ready heart to receive!

Dear Lord Jesus, I believe in my heart and confess with my mouth that you are the Son of the living God! Please forgive me for all my past, present, and future sins. I ask for you to come into my heart and save me and change me into the person you would have me to be. Thank you for all you did for me by shedding your blood and dying on the cross. I believe God raised you from the dead, and I receive you as my Lord and Savior. In Jesus name, Amen!

For those who confessed that prayer with a sincere heart, congratulations, and welcome to the family of God! God's Holy Spirit will teach, lead, comfort, and guide you as He begins to transform you into His likeness. As you continue in your walk with God, you will begin to see yourself changing for the good. Most importantly, you are now born-again and saved for all eternity! Please find yourself a Bible-teaching church so you can begin to learn and grow in the Word of God.

ABOUT THE AUTHOR

Jacqui D. Williams-Skipwith is the author of four books: *How Do I Know I Am Really Saved?*, *The Importance of Tithes and Offerings*, *God Is Speaking to You*, and *Life after Death: Heaven and Hell Are Real Places*. Her primary mission and objective in writing quick reference handbooks is to give the reader a brief glimpse into the knowledge and understanding of God's Word and to increase their desire for a better relationship with Him. Through her writings, she shares her life experiences from the topics given to her by the direction of the Holy Spirit of God.

You may purchase the author's books on:

Amazon, Barnes and Noble, Apple iTunes,
and various other platforms

View the author's pages on:

www.amazon.com/author/jacquidwilliams
www.goodreads.com

Your feedback is welcomed!